Penetration Testing Services
Procurement Guide

Penetration Testing Services Procurement Guide

Published by:
CREST
Tel: 0845 686-5542
Email: **admin@crest-approved.org**

Principal Author
Jason Creasey,
Managing Director, Jerakano Limited

Principal reviewer
Ian Glover, President, CREST

Acknowledgements

CREST would like to extend its special thanks to those CREST member organisations who took part in interviews and to those clients who agreed to be case studies.

Warning

DTP notes

For ease of reference, the following DTP devices have been used throughout the procurement Guide.

 A Good Tip

 A Timely Warning

 An insightful Project Finding

Quotes are presented in blue italics, like this.

TABLE OF CONTENTS

A STRUCTURED APPROACH FOR PROCURING PENETRATION TESTING SERVICES

Stage A – Determine the business requirements for testing

- Overview
- Evaluate the drivers for conducting a penetration test
- Identify target environment
- Define the purpose of the penetration test
- Produce requirements specification

Stage B – Agree testing scope

- Overview
- Determine testing style (eg. black, grey or white box testing)
- Agree testing type (eg. web application or infrastructure testing)
- Identify testing constraints
- Produce scope statement

Stage C – Establish a management assurance framework

- The need for a management assurance framework
- Establish an assurance process
- Define and agree contracts
- Understand and mitigate risks
- Introduce change management
- Agree a problem resolution approach

Stage D – Plan and conduct testing

- Overview
- Carry out planning
- Conduct research

- Identify vulnerabilities
- Exploit weaknesses
- Report findings
- Remediate issues

Stage E – Implement improvement programme

- Overview
- Address root causes of weaknesses
- Evaluate penetration testing effectiveness
- Identify lessons learned
- Apply good practice enterprise-wide
- Create and monitor an action plan
- Agree approach for future testing

PART I: INTRODUCTION AND OVERVIEW

About this Guide

This *Procurement Guide* (the Guide) provides practical advice on the purchase and management of penetration testing services, helping you to conduct effective, value-for-money penetration testing. It is designed to enable your organisation to plan for a penetration test, select an appropriate third party provider and manage all important related activities.

The Guide presents a useful overview of the key concepts you will need to understand to conduct a well-managed penetration test, explaining what a penetration test is (and is not), outlining its' strengths and limitations, and describing why an organisation would typically choose to employ an external provider of penetration testing services.

✅ While the main focus of this report is to help organisations procure penetration services from external suppliers, it will also be useful for organisations who decide to undertake penetration tests themselves.

Presented as a useful five stage procurement approach, the Guide then provides advice and guidance on how to:

1. *Determine business requirements for a penetration test,* considering the drivers for testing, the purpose of testing and target environments.
2. *Agree the testing scope,* approving testing style and type and assessing testing constraints.
3. *Establish a management framework* to assure quality, reduce risk, manage changes and problems and agree contract.
4. *Plan and conduct the penetration test itself,* which consists of conducting research, identifying vulnerabilities, exploiting weaknesses, report finding and remediating issues.
5. *Implement an improvement programme* to address weaknesses, identify lessons learned, instigate actions and agree an approach for future testing.

Finally, the Guide highlights the main criteria to consider when choosing an appropriate external provider of penetration testing services (referred to as 'the supplier'). The six key selection criteria for choosing a suitable supplier of penetration testing services are highlighted in *Figure 1* and explored in more detail *in Part 4 – Choosing a suitable supplier.*

1. Solid reputation, history and ethics
2. High quality, value-for-money services
3. Research and development capability
4. Highly competent, technical testers
5. Security and risk management
6. Strong professional accreditation and complaint process

Figure 1: Key selection criteria for choosing a suitable supplier of penetration testing services

Purpose

The purpose of the Procurement Guide is to help you to:

- Understand objectives for conducting a penetration test;
- Gain an overview of the key components of an effective penetration testing approach;
- Determine whether or not to conduct a penetration test;
- Assess the need to outsource the undertaking of a penetration test;
- Identify what needs to be considered when planning for a penetration test;
- Consider the different types of penetration tests that are available;
- Learn about the penetration testing process – and associated methodologies;
- Determine criteria upon which to base selection of an appropriate supplier.

Scope

This Guide is focused on helping your organisation to choose the right supplier, at the right time, for the right reasons. This Guide is designed to help organisations procure penetration services from external suppliers, but will also be useful for organisations conducting penetration tests themselves.

✅ There are often special requirements for penetration testing service providers, for example when supplying services to UK Government departments. Organisations supplying services must have CHECK 'green light' clearance from CESG. Although these specific requirements are out of scope for this guide, they are typically covered by the contents of this Guide anyway. Further information on CHECK can be found at: *www.cesg.gov.uk/site/check/index.cfm*.

Rationale

Organisations have the evolving task of securing complex IT environments whilst delivering their business and brand objectives. The threat to key systems is ever increasing; the probability of a security weakness being accidentally exposed or maliciously exploited needs to be continually assessed – such as via a penetration test – to ensure that the level of risk is at an acceptable level to the business.

Much of the material in this Guide is based on the findings of a research project – conducted by Jerakano Limited on behalf of CREST – about the main requirements organisations have for considering and conducting penetration tests. One of the main reasons for commissioning a research project was that the customers of CREST members were often unclear about how to best procure penetration testing services.

✅ A summary of CREST activities can be found at *www.crest-approved.org/*. Where relevant, CREST benefits are also highlighted throughout the Guide.

🔎 For ease of use, where key points in this document refer to the findings of the research project, they are signposted by one of these *'Project Finding'* boxes.

The research project was based on:

- Reviews of relevant material produced by industry bodies, including CPNI, OWASP, OSSTM and PTES (see following *Tip* and *Appendix C* for more details);
- Desktop (mainly web-based) research;
- Analysis of responses to a questionnaire about various topics associated with procuring penetration testing services;
- Interviews with leading suppliers of penetration testing services;

- Case studies of major client organisations.

✅ Some of the principle sources of material reviewed included:
- The *Open Source Security Testing Methodology Manual (OSSTMM)* from ISECOM;
- The *Open Web Application Security project (OWASP)* from the OWASP foundation;
- The *Penetration Testing Execution Standard (PTES),* being produced by a group of information security practitioners from all areas of the industry;
- The *Best Practice Guide – Commercial available penetration testing* from the centre for the protection of national infrastructure (CPNI).

Audience

Historically, mainly due to legal or regulatory requirements, many organisations requiring penetration tests have come from government departments, utilities (eg. gas, water or telecoms), pharmaceuticals, banks and other financial institutions. However, an increasing array of organisations now conduct penetration testing, not just for compliance reasons but because of the on-line nature of nearly all businesses today and the increasing threat from real (often cyber) attacks. Consequently, this Guide has been designed to apply to all market sectors.

The main audience for this guide is individuals who are involved in the procurement of penetration testing services.

🔎 Findings from the research project were that the main individuals likely to read a Guide of this type would be:
1. Procurement specialists
2. IT project management
3. IT system or application
4. Compliance officers
5. Internal or external auditors
6. Business managers

The most likely individual to read this Guide – and to be responsible for procuring penetration testing services – is a Procurement specialist. However, it can be very difficult for them to ask the right questions. In addition to traditional procurement questions (concerning company structure, history and process), organisations should also consider the competence of the individual penetration testers, the scope of the testing, methods and tools used, security of information being accessed and the potential compromise of systems and data. Consequently, organisations are advised to involve other relevant departments (eg. IT and security) in the procurement of penetration testing providers.

PART II: UNDERSTANDING THE KEY CONCEPTS

Introduction

Penetration testing is not a straightforward process. It is often very technical in nature – and riddled with jargon – which can make it look daunting to organisations considering the need to undertake it.

⚠ There are many buzzwords that can be associated with penetration testing (rightly and wrongly) including ethical hacking; tiger teaming; vulnerability analysis; and security testing, assessment or assurance.

There are many questions organisations may ask themselves when considering the need for penetration testing, which can include:
- What exactly is a penetration test, and how does is it differ to other types of security techniques?
- What are the compelling reasons to perform a penetration test?
- Who should conduct the test?
- How do we go about it?
- What are the risks and constraints that we should be concerned about?
- How do we decide which supplier to choose?

This part of the Guide presents a high-level response to these questions, while the remainder of the report explores responses to them in more detail.

Definition of a penetration test

Penetration testing involves the use of a variety of manual and automated techniques to simulate an attack on an organisation's information security arrangements.

It should be conducted by a qualified and independent penetration testing expert, sometimes referred to as an ethical security tester. Penetration testing looks to exploit known vulnerabilities but should also use the expertise of the tester to identify specific weaknesses – unknown vulnerabilities – in an organisation's security arrangements.

A penetration test, occasionally *pen test*, is a method of evaluating the security of a computer system or network by simulating an attack from malicious outsiders (who do not have an authorised means of accessing the organisation's systems) and/or malicious insiders (who have some level of authorised access).

The penetration testing process involves an active analysis of the target system for any potential vulnerabilities that could result from poor or improper system configuration, both known and unknown hardware or software flaws, and operational weaknesses in process or technical countermeasures. This analysis is typically carried out from the position of a potential attacker and can involve active exploitation of security vulnerabilities.

A Penetration Test is typically an assessment of IT infrastructure, networks and business applications to identify attack vectors, vulnerabilities and control weaknesses.

Findings from the research project revealed that the two most common forms of penetration testing are:
• Application penetration testing (typically web applications), which finds technical vulnerabilities;
• Infrastructure penetration testing, which examines servers, firewalls and other hardware for security vulnerabilities.

Other forms of penetration testing are also popular, which include:
• mobile application penetration testing;
• client server (or legacy) application penetration testing;
• device penetration testing, (including workstations, laptops and consumer devices (eg. tablets and smartphones);
• wireless penetration testing;
• telephony or VoIP penetration testing.

The penetration testing process typically includes: conducting research and identifying vulnerabilities; exploiting weaknesses; reporting findings; and remediating issues. Each of these steps is explored in *Stage D Undertaking a penetration test.*

Technical security testing

Penetration testing has been in use for many years and is one of a range of ways for testing the technical security of a system.

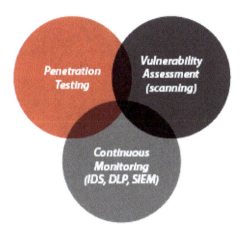

Figure 2: Technical security weakness discovery techniques

Penetration testing can easily be confused with other forms of technical security testing, particularly Vulnerability Assessment. In some cases, there can also be a relationship with continuous monitoring services (eg. intrusion detection or prevention systems and Data Loss Prevention (DLP) technology or processes). The way in which these three types of technical security services overlap is shown in *Figure 2*.

Vulnerability Assessments
Vulnerability assessment (sometimes referred to as 'scanning') is the use of automated tools to identify known common vulnerabilities in a system's configuration. Vulnerability Assessment tools scan the information systems environment to establish whether security settings have been switched on and consistently applied – and that appropriate security patches have been deployed.

Vulnerability assessment typically seeks to validate the minimum level of security that should be applied – and is often the pre-cursor to more specialised penetration testing. It does not exploit the vulnerabilities identified to replicate a real attack, nor does it consider the overall security management processes and procedures that support the system.

A penetration test is an ethical attack simulation that is intended to demonstrate or validate the effectiveness of security controls in a particular environment by highlighting risks posed by actual exploitable vulnerabilities. It is built around a manual testing process, which is intended to go much further than the generic responses, false positive findings and lack of depth provided by automated application assessment tools (such as those used in a vulnerability assessment).

Penetration testing in context

Penetration testing should be placed in the context of security management as a whole. To gain an appropriate level of assurance, a range of reviews should be conducted. These are often aligned to standards such as ISO27001, COBIT or the ISF Standard of Good Practice. Whilst these standards reference penetration testing, they only do it from a management perspective.

Most existing security management standards do not describe penetration testing in any depth, nor do they put the testing strategy in context. Consequently, systems and environments that comply with these standards may not be technically secure. A balanced approach of technical and non-technical testing should therefore be taken to ensure the overall integrity of security controls.

There are many forms of testing – ideally performed by an independent (often external) team – that help to provide appropriate levels of information security assurance. These include technical reviews of applications development and implementation standards; security reviews of the Information Security Management System (ISMS) and compliance audits.

✔ While other forms of security assurance provide only a theoretical articulation of vulnerability, penetration testing demonstrates actual vulnerability against defined and real threats. As such the results from a penetration test can be more compelling and demonstrable to both senior management and technical staff.

Assurance cannot be gained from any one of these activities in isolation and penetration testing has a key role to play. It is also important to consider how testing is built into the systems development lifecycle activities and that regular testing can provide an industry benchmark against which the improvements in the technical security environment can be measured.

'Organisations should not describe themselves as secure – there are only varying degrees of insecurity'

Penetration testing limitations

Undertaking a series of penetration tests will help test some of your security arrangements and identify improvements, but it is not a panacea for all ills. For example, a penetration test:

- covers just the target application, infrastructure or environment that has been selected;
- focuses on the exposures in technical infrastructure, so is not intended to cover all ways in which critical or sensitive information could leak out of your organisation;
- plays only a small part (despite often including social engineering tests) in reviewing the people element (often the most important element of an organisation's defence system);
- is only a snapshot of a system at a point in time;
- can be limited by legal or commercial considerations, limiting the breadth or depth of a test;
- may not uncover all security weaknesses, for example due to a restricted scope or inadequate testing;
- provides results that are often technical in nature and need to be interpreted in a business context.

Penetration tests will need to supplement a full range of security management activities, including those laid out in ISO27001 or the ISF Standard of Good Practice.

The buyers challenge

In addition to the penetration testing limitations highlighted above, many organisations are facing a number of more general challenges when carrying out penetration testing.

Findings from the research project indicated that the top six challenges for buyers included difficulties in:

1. Determining the depth and breadth of coverage of the test;
2. Identifying what type of penetration test is required;
3. Understanding the difference between vulnerability scanning and penetration testing;
4. Identifying risks associated with potential system failure and exposure of sensitive data;
5. Agreeing the targets and frequency of tests;
6. Assuming that by fixing vulnerabilities uncovered during a penetration test their systems will then be 'secure'.

Other challenges for buyers can include difficulties in:

- Establishing a business case for a test to be undertaken;
- Understanding the costs of external services – and in determining the true overall cost;
- Remediating system vulnerabilities effectively;
- Finding a suitable penetration testing expert when required (eg. at short notice).

In order for these challenges to be identified and addressed effectively, an organisation should adopt a systematic, structured approach to penetration testing, including the selection and management of external suppliers.

Using external suppliers

Organisations can carry out penetration testing themselves, sometimes very successfully. More often they will decide to employ the services of one or more specialist third party penetration testing providers.

There are many reasons why an organisation may wish to employ external penetration testing providers, such as to help meet the challenges outlined in the previous section.

Findings from the research project indicated that the top three reasons (by some way) why organisations hire external suppliers are because these suppliers can:

1. Provide more experienced, dedicated technical staff who understand how to carry out penetration tests effectively;
2. Perform an independent assessment of their security arrangements;
3. Carry out a full range of testing (eg. black, white or grey box; internal or external; infrastructure or web application; source code review; and social engineering).

Other reasons given for using external suppliers are because they can:

- Deploy a structured process and plan, developed by experts;
- Increase the scope and frequency of tests;
- Conduct short term engagements, eliminating the need to employ your own specialised (and often expensive) staff – and reducing the cost of training (and re-training) internal teams;
- Take advantage of automation (eg. penetration testing workflows, importing vulnerability management reports).

There are many benefits in procuring penetration testing services from a trusted, certified external company who employ professional, ethical and highly technically competent individuals. CREST member companies are certified penetration testing organisations who fully meet these requirements, having been awarded the gold standard in penetration testing, building trusted relationships with their clients.

Conclusions

When carried out and reported properly, a penetration test can give you knowledge of nearly all of your technical security weaknesses and provide you with the information and support required to fix those vulnerabilities. There are also other significant benefits to the organisation through effective penetration testing, which can include:

- A reduction in your ICT costs over the long term;
- Improvements in the technical environment, reducing support calls;

- Greater levels of confidence in the security of your IT environments;
- Increased awareness of the need for appropriate technical controls.

However, there can be many tricky issues that need to be addressed before conducting a penetration test, to ensure that requirements are being properly defined and met. There are also limitations and risks that need to be identified and managed. Consequently, it should be considered essential to adopt a systematic, structured approach when carrying out a penetration test – and in selecting an appropriate supplier.

Although value can be obtained by appointing either certified testers or certified organisations, it is the combination of these that will provide you with the greatest assurance that the most effective tests will be conducted – and in the most professional manner.

Furthermore, by procuring penetration testing services from certified testers who work for certified organisations (as CREST require), you can rest assured that an expert and independent body – with real authority – is on hand to investigate any complaint thoroughly and ensure that a satisfactory conclusion is reached

If you want to know more about:
- The five key stages of an effective approach for conducting a penetration test, please read *Part 3 – Adopting a systematic, structured approach to penetration testing.*
- A practical method of identifying and selecting an appropriate supplier, please read *Part 4 – Choosing a suitable supplier.*

'It is important to ensure that the right systems are being tested by the right people for the right reasons at the right time'

PART III: ADOPTING A STRUCTURED APPROACH TO PENETRATION TESTING

Overview

When performing penetration tests, some organisations adopt an ad hoc or piecemeal approach, often depending on the needs of a particular region, business unit – or the IT department. Whilst this can meet some specific requirements, this approach is unlikely to provide real assurance about the security condition of your systems enterprise-wide.

Consequently, it is often more effective to adopt a more systematic, structured approach to penetration testing, ensuring that:

- Business requirements are met.
- Major system vulnerabilities are identified and addressed.
- Risks are kept within business parameters.

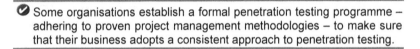 Some organisations establish a formal penetration testing programme – adhering to proven project management methodologies – to make sure that their business adopts a consistent approach to penetration testing.

To help you make the most of your penetration testing, a procurement approach has been developed and is presented in *Figure 3*. The five stages in this approach are described in more detail in the remainder of this part of the Guide.

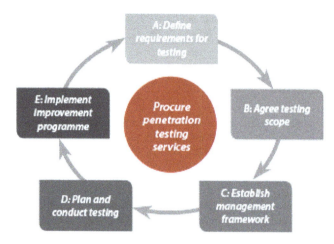

Figure 3: A structured approach to penetration testing

Many organisations choose to appoint a trusted, specialist organisation (a CREST member), employing qualified professionals (CREST qualified staff), to help them conduct penetration tests. Although suppliers can be brought in just to conduct testing, they can also help with any of the activities outlined above. Typically, suppliers are appointed during or just after *Stage A – Define requirements for testing.*

Before deciding which supplier to select, an organisation should become familiar with the main activities in each of the five stages.

Overview

There will often be a trigger that causes you to carry out a penetration test (or a series of tests), possibly due to being informed about a need for compliance or as a result of an incident affecting your organisation (or a similar organisation).

It can be tempting to immediately start thinking about getting an external supplier to just come in and start testing.

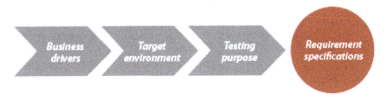

Figure 4: A process for specifying penetration testing requirements

But in reality, a more effective approach is to determine your business requirements for penetration testing first, and then consider the best way that these requirements can be met. The key elements of a possible approach are shown in *Figure 4*.

Evaluate the drivers for conducting a penetration test

Organisations can have many different drivers for undertaking penetration tests of their critical business applications or infrastructure.

Findings from the research project revealed that the four main drivers for penetration testing include a high degree of concern about:

1. A growing requirement for compliance;
2. The impact of serious (often cyber related) security attacks on other similar organisations;
3. Use of a greater number and variety of outsourced services;
4. Significant changes to business processes.

Whatever the drivers are for testing in your organisation, it is important to determine what it is that penetration testing will help you to achieve.

✅ One supplier interviewed explained that often the main drivers for customers carrying out penetration tests were to:

- Raise awareness of security and the threats that could come to fruition;
- Prove compliance with legal or regulatory requirements;
- Reinforce their technical security competence.

When determining requirements for a penetration test, you should also take into account a number of other topics, such as:

- How a penetration test fits into your organisation's overall security arrangements;
- The nature and direction of your business – and your risk appetite;
- Findings from risk assessments, audits or reviews carried out by specialists in information security assessments, risk management, business continuity, internal audit or insurance;
- Overall compliance requirements, not just those directly mentioning penetration tests;
- Analysis of security incidents that have taken place both in your own organisation and in similar organisations;
- Lessons learnt from any previous penetration tests conducted within your organisation.

✅ Penetration tests carried out in isolation can derive a good understanding of technical risks and identify security improvements. However, if the testing can be placed within a wider framework of security assessment and strategy it will help to contextualise the findings and recommendations. It should also help to ensure that a more strategic view of security management is adopted, reducing the risk of discovering that the same problems still exits (or exists on a similar system) the next time a penetration test is carried out.

Identify target systems

An organisation will need to identify the target system or systems to be tested, such as a standard business application; a specialised web application; a key part of infrastructure; or a data centre.

Findings from the research project revealed that when identifying target systems, the main criteria typically considered are:

1. The criticality of the system to the organisation (often identified by performing a criticality or risk assessment);
2. Compliance requirements (eg. PCI DSS);
3. Major business or IT changes;
4. Critical systems under development;
5. Outsourced applications or infrastructure (including cloud services).

Criticality

To identify their most critical systems, organisations would typically consider the:
- nature of the business being conducted;
- size of the target systems – and the sensitivity of data associated with the systems;
- potential business impact if that system were to be compromised – and the likelihood of the system actually becoming compromised.

For some organisations, the first step in procuring a penetration test is to carry out a risk assessment of an organisation's assets. This helps to ensure that the testing planned will focus on the assets which pose the highest risk to the organisation.

Compliance

Some industries and types of data are regulated and must be handled securely (like the financial sector or credit card data). In this case, your regulator will insist on a penetration test as part of a certification process. Some industry standards, such as ISO27001 and PCI DSS, also specify the requirement for penetration testing.

'Compliance is a different beast to security and exists separately from security. It is possible to be compliant, yet not secure; and relatively secure, but non-compliant'

Major changes

Most organisations in today's dynamic world make significant changes on a fairly regular basis, be they to business processes, applications, IT systems or end user environments, many of which can have a significant impact on the threat profile of an organisation and the security arrangements they have in place. Consequently, it can be important to carry out a penetration test of a system immediately following a major change to the system itself or the business environment it supports.

Systems under development

Often the decision to conduct independent penetration testing on a new system comes late in the project lifecycle and the result is often insufficient budget for desired testing, very limited time before the system needs to go live and little ability to change the system as a result of any security vulnerabilities identified.

Security testing should be fully incorporated into your system development lifecycle (SDLC) – as outlined in the following table– and not just conducted as a 'tick box' exercise at the end.

SDLC stage	Actions to consider	..to ensure that....
1. Planning and requirements	Build independent penetration testing into requirement specifications – allocating sufficient funding and resources – and schedule at key points in the plan.	Business and security requirements are met.
2. Design	Engage with penetration testing supplier to define scope and incorporate this in to your project plan – and to conduct threat modelling exercises.	Penetration testing is baked into the design process.
3. Development	Integrate penetration tests into your traditional security testing approaches, including source code review.	Coding weaknesses are identified as soon as possible.
4. Integration and test	Perform vulnerability scanning and build reviews.	System builds are secure.
5. Implementation	Conduct exploitation testing of applications and networks.	Vulnerabilities are addressed.
6. Maintenance	Subject critical systems to regular penetration testing (at least yearly) – and after any major change.	Systems continue to be as well protected as possible.

Outsourcing

Many organisations place a great deal of reliance on services they have outsourced (often to cloud service providers), but an attacker is not constrained to whether the business manages its own environment or not. Any weaknesses in the security of these third parties can significantly impact on the integrity of an organisation's IT security.

If you are not permitted to test an important environment controlled by a third party you should seek assurances that:

• Appropriate penetration tests are regularly carried out;
• These tests are conducted by suitably qualified staff working for a certified organisation;
• Recommendations from the tests are acted upon.

Define the purpose of the test

Having determined the target system for the penetration test, be it for a web application, a data centre or an outsourced service, you should identify the specific purpose for carrying out a particular penetration test.

Results from the research project revealed that the main business purpose for conducting a penetration test of a particular environment is to help an organisation:

1. Identify weaknesses in their security controls;
2. Enable the business (particularly for electronic commerce);
3. Reduce the frequency and impact of security incidents;
4. Comply with legal and regulatory requirements (eg. PCI / DSS, NERC, ISO27001, HIPAA or FISMA);
5. Provide assurance to third parties that business applications can be trusted and that customer data is adequately protected.

'We suspected that we had already been hacked, and wanted to find out more about the threats to our systems, to help reduce the risk of another successful attack.'

⊘ Another purpose for conducting a penetration test can be to limit liabilities if things go wrong, or if there is a court case (ie. take 'reasonable' precautions) – referred to by some interviewees as 'covering your back'.

Produce a requirements specification

Requirements for a penetration test should be formally recorded in a requirements specification, which should include the:

- business drivers for the test, including security and reporting requirements;
- target environment(s) to be tested;
- purpose of the test;
- budget and resources available;
- timing of the test;
- roles and responsibilities.

Once the requirements specification is produced – and often before – most organisations are typically ready to select an appropriate supplier to help them plan, prepare for and conduct the test.

⊘ Details about how to select an appropriate supplier can be found in *Part 4 Choosing a supplier.*

Overview

Prior to commencement of testing activities, the scope of the penetration test will need to be defined. This scope – often undertaken with the chosen testing supplier – should be dependent on the target environment to be tested and the business purpose for conducting the test, as defined in the requirements specification.

The key elements associated with defining the scope of any testing to be performed are outlined in *Figure 5*.

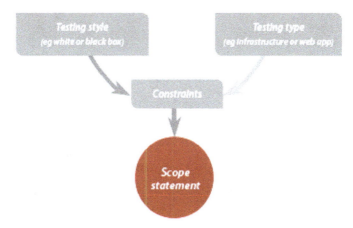

Figure 5: Key elements in the production of a scope statement

Some scoping activities will encompass multiple types of test. For example, a test of a web site may include an infrastructure test of the web site hardware, software and network devices as well as an application level test of the web site code itself.

It is important to determine which systems are 'out of scope'. For example, a web site being tested may use an e-mail service for messaging, but testing this service may not be considered part of the scope. These 'out of scope' systems should be specified to prevent ambiguity in the testing scope, which could result in incomplete coverage or unauthorised testing (possibly leading to an outage).

When defining the scope, you should be aware that testing just the technical implementation of an application in isolation will not uncover management or operational vulnerabilities. By testing the associated people, policies and processes, issues can be identified – and addressed – that could cause defects in the technology, reducing the risk of systems being compromised later.

Style of testing

Careful consideration should be given to the style of testing that is required, such as black, grey or white box testing, as outlined in the following table.

Testing style	Overview	Useful to...
'Black box'	No information is provided to the penetration tester	Simulate external attacks with no prior knowledge of the target environment – and understand what is possible for an uninformed attacker to achieve.
'Grey box', also known as 'translucent box'	Limited information is provided, eg. login credentials to a system or visitor access to a site	Understand the degree of access that authorised users of a system can obtain – and the possible damage caused by insider or privileged attacks with some knowledge of the target environment.
'White box' – also known as 'crystal or oblique box'	Full information is provided, eg. network maps and access to development staff	Support a more targeted test on a system that requires a test of as many vulnerabilities and attack vectors as possible.

White box testing can be less authentic as an attack, but is much more effective use of a penetration tester's time, reducing cost to your business.

Findings from the research project revealed that the majority of suppliers' clients specify white or grey box testing, rather than black box testing. Many clients simply ask a supplier to run a 'typical' penetration test, which is nearly always involves grey box testing.

The more traditional black box testing is still undertaken, but this tends to be for a specific purpose.

Black box testing can be a little misleading. For some system attacks, a determined attacker would do so much reconnaissance that they would have virtually the same knowledge as an insider anyway

Testing can be carried out either at a supplier's premises or at a client's location (or a little of both).
- An 'external' penetration test is the most common type of test and is aimed at IT systems from 'outside the building', testing systems that are 'internet connected', such as the DMZ of your network, VPN and your web sites.
- An internal security test (sometimes replicated by a supplier on their own site, maybe in a laboratory) focuses on what staff can see and do within their own IT network, and is typically associated with white or grey box testing.

Type of testing

The scope of the test should identify what type of testing is to be performed, such as web application testing (which finds coding vulnerabilities), or infrastructure testing (which examines servers, firewalls and other hardware for security vulnerabilities).

Some organisations classify applications (in terms of criticality) as high, medium or low value applications – and test accordingly. Infrastructure testing is often carried out on a regular cycle or after a major change.

Other forms of system penetration testing are also conducted such as for mobile, client server or cloud-based applications; user devices, including workstations, laptops and consumer devices (eg. tablets and smartphones); and wireless – but typically the same penetration testing principles apply.

For optimum results, the penetration test should be conducted in the live environment. However, this not always possible (or advisable), so testing is often carried out in a 'test' environment.

✅ Testing activities conducted in a 'test' environment:

- Allow more disruptive or destructive testing tests to be performed, such as 'denial of service' type tests or the use of exploits against vulnerabilities;
- Are unlikely to affect users of 'live' systems, so there will be no business impact;
- Should be as similar to the live environment as possible.

Testing constraints

There are always constraints with any form of testing and penetration testing is no exception. Tests are often constrained by legal, operational, logistical or financial requirements – magnified by a lack of time and resources to carry out extensive testing on a continuous basis. Testing constraints need to be identified and adhered to, whilst ensuring real world scenarios are adequately tested.

The following table outlines common penetration testing restrictions, highlighting the potential implications for malicious attackers and presenting actions to consider for addressing these issues.

Constraint on tester	Implication for attackers	Actions to consider
There are typically aspects of the business that cannot be tested due to operational limitations.	Attackers often do whatever it takes to penetrate an organisation or system. If they are not able to penetrate a particular system, they may simply try another route.	Simulate live tests as closely as possible. Conduct tests outside of normal hours (and locations).
Testing must be conducted within the confines of the law.	Attackers will often break the law to achieve their objectives.	Tailor the way tests are structured and run to simulate most forms of attack. Take back-ups of critical systems and files before testing.

Constraint on tester	Implication for attackers	Actions to consider
Testers are limited to the scope of the testing – they are unlikely to be allowed to utilise business partners, customers or service providers as a platform from which to launch an attack.	Attackers will utilise the weakest point of security in any part of connected systems or networks to mount an attack, regardless of ownership, location or jurisdiction.	Include perimeter controls within the scope of the test. Apply more rigorous testing to applications that are accessible from outside the boundaries of the business.
Limited time to conduct tests.	Attackers have unlimited time to mount a concerted attack against a system if they have the motivation, capability and resources to do so.	Invest more time in testing critical systems. Provide testers with as much background information as possible, reducing reconnaissance time and thereby increasing testing time.
Any test is only a snap shot in time, and changes to the threat or the environment could introduce new vulnerabilities.	Attackers can attack the environment at any time.	Conduct penetration testing on a regular basis, rather than as a one-off exercise.

Bearing in mind these testing constraints, penetration testing should not be assumed to find all vulnerabilities of a given system. The law of diminishing returns often applies in that the most obvious vulnerabilities will be discovered first, with further time yielding more and more obscure issues. Consequently, it is often advisable to adopt a 'risk to cost balance' when performing tests.

🔴 Simply fixing vulnerabilities uncovered during testing could leave a number of other vulnerabilities present for an attacker to find – emphasising the need to employ competent professional penetration testers.

Technical considerations

To carry out the most effective penetration testing the environment being tested should be as close to the live environment as possible. However, there are often technical issues that need to be considered that can affect the scope of the test or the security countermeasures in place to detect and deter attacks. As an example, two of the most common of these technical considerations are outlined in the following table:

If you have......	You may need to......
IDS/IPS deployed within your environment.	Implement policy exceptions and ensure that they do not significantly block the testing.
Network or web application firewalls deployed.	Be aware that vulnerabilities present in your servers or application will not be discovered if the testing is undertaken from outside your network.

There may be many other technical considerations that are specific to your environment. However, the key points to remember are that you should:

- Define how the testing will be conducted during the scoping phase;

- Ensure that the scope is practical and that the testing will meet your requirements.

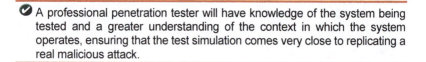 A professional penetration tester will have knowledge of the system being tested and a greater understanding of the context in which the system operates, ensuring that the test simulation comes very close to replicating a real malicious attack.

Reporting formats

Effective reporting is a critical aspect of penetration testing and its importance is often overlooked. The format and content of reporting should be defined in both the scope and in a formal contract.

Depending on the test objective, you should ensure that your supplier will:

- Provide a detailed technical report on the vulnerabilities of the system;

- Explain the vulnerabilities in a way that is understandable by senior management;

- Report the outcome of the test in business risk terms;
- Identify short term (tactical) recommendations;
- Conclude with and define 'root cause' long term (strategic) recommendations;
- Include a security improvement action plan;
- Provide assistance to the organisation in implementing the security improvements.

---

❷ A good report will include the names, roles and qualifications of the testers; date of the report; type of test undertaken; and test scope. It should highlight any issues affecting the validity of the results and any other unknowns or anomalies encountered during testing.

Whilst reports need to be made to a technical audience, an executive summary is often essential – presenting the results in a business risk context; highlighting particular concerns, identifying patterns and providing a high-level statement of the required corrective action.

---

❷ On-going communication during tests can take the form of regular updates, supported by alerts if a serious vulnerability has been discovered.

Produce the scope statement

The scope of the test should be recorded in a formal document and signed off by authorised individuals from all relevant parties.

The following table outlines the type of element that would typically be included in the scope statement. This information will need to be disseminated within the organisation, for example to operations staff who may mistakenly report testing activities as actual attacks on the organisation.

Scoping element	Considerations
Definition of target environment	• Which systems are in and out of scope. • The testing approach being adopted (eg. black, white or grey box). • Types of test that are prohibited (eg. 'denial of service' type testing). • Where the testing team will need to be in order to conduct the testing (eg. on the customer's site or at the test supplier's premises). • Approvals required for the testing to go ahead.
Resourcing requirements	• Who will be leading the testing engagement. • The names of testers that will be used for the testing engagement, with details about their roles, skills, experience, qualifications and backgrounds. • The number of days required – and the days when testing will take place.
Report requirements	• The format of the test report (template often used). • When the test report will be delivered (not later than a few days after completion of the test). • How the test report will be delivered (electronic and / or physical).
Communication processes	• Information and resources that the testers will need prior to testing. • How affected third parties will be informed and consulted in relation to testing activities. • How testing start-up and close-down will be covered. • Regular (often daily) communications (eg. teleconferences or meetings).
Liabilities of both parties	• Steps required by both parties should problems (eg. slippage) arise. • Details of liability (indemnity) insurance held by the testing supplier.
Follow up activities	• Presentation of the report to senior management. • Re-testing activities once mitigations have been made for the discovered vulnerabilities.

❶ The penetration tester must be authorised to perform any tests on your systems, which can often be achieved by formally defining what is to be tested and how it will be tested. The test team will also require a disclaimer stating that they are legally authorised to carry out specified activity on your property and systems.

The need for a management assurance framework

Once the scope has been defined, some organisations leave the supplier to conduct penetration testing with little further interaction. However, this may not result in optimum or desired results being obtained and can lead to significant difficulties if problems arise either with the testing itself or with the way in which the test is conducted.

Consequently, it is important to establish a management assurance framework to help manage the testing process. An effective framework will provide assurance to stakeholders that:

- The objectives of the penetration test(s) are achieved (ie. business requirements are met);
- Contracts with suppliers are defined, agreed, signed off and monitored;
- Risks to the organisation (eg. degradation or loss of services, disclosure of sensitive information) are kept to a minimum;
- Any changes to the scope of the penetration test (eg. additional testing requested, such as to include wireless or device testing) or to organisational controls (eg. to address a critical weakness uncovered during testing) are managed quickly and efficiently;
- Problems (and complaints) arising during the test (eg. due to resources not being made available, tests not working as planned or an ethical breach) are satisfactorily resolved.

Key components of a management assurance framework

The key elements of a management assurance framework for penetration testing are shown in *Figure 6*, with each element being described on the following pages.

Figure 6: A management assurance formwork for penetration testing

Ideally, you as the client should establish and control the management assurance framework. Your supplier should be aware of these needs and help you build this framework, but responsibility for the actual systems and data – and any assurance about them – rests with your organisation.

Assurance process

To ensure that a penetration testing process meets requirements, it is important that all aspects of a penetration testing project (which includes determining requirements; carrying out planning and preparation; and performing the actual tests) are managed effectively. Consequently, your organisation should establish an assurance process to oversee the testing, monitoring performance against requirements and ensuring appropriate actions are being taken

✔ An effective management assurance framework will establish control processes over all important management aspects of testing, such as:

- Test administration (eg. scope; legal constraints; disclosure; and reporting);
- Test execution (eg. approach; separation of systems and duties; tool heritage; traceability and repeatability of tests);
- Data security (eg. secure storage, transmission, processing and destruction of critical or sensitive information provided or accessed during the test; the results of the test; and recommended actions).

Contract definition

It is important that the scope of the test is clearly defined in a legally binding contract, signed off by all relevant parties before testing starts.

❗ The contract should always be referred to a legal team to ensure that the terms of business and the detail of the contract and schedule of work are acceptable, as suppliers often:

- Caveat risks to your organisation (and theirs);
- Require you to acknowledge that you understand penetration testing involves an element of risk;
- Seek indemnities from you for work that they undertake.

As well as the scope of the testing to be undertaken, the contract should also include:

- explicit exclusions (eg. systems that are out of scope);
- technical and operational constraints;
- roles and responsibilities for all parties concerned;
- specific legal and regulatory requirements;
- timings and checkpoints;
- a problem escalation process;
- reporting and presentation style;
- post-test corrective action strategy and action plan development;
- pricing and terms of business.

✅ You should consider requiring your supplier to:

- Nominate a senior manager (who can be easily contacted during the testing process) to be accountable for managing the delivery of the test;
- Clearly explain the limits and dangers of the security test as part of the statement of work;
- Provide confidentiality and non-disclosure of customer information and test results.

Risk mitigation

Performing any sort of penetration test carries with it some risk to the target system and the business information associated with it. Risks to the organisation (eg. degradation or loss of services, disclosure of sensitive information) need to be kept to a minimum. These risks can be reduced by advanced planning, clear definition of scope and predefined escalation procedures.

❗ Some tests are carried out without the full knowledge of those responsible for the running of the systems, which can result in unexpected business consequences, such as an inadvertent trigger of internal controls. Consequently, all affected operational areas should be informed and/or an escalation process established. Relevant management must be available during the test period to ensure testing takes place as agreed and risks remain within acceptable boundaries, to deal with any problems arising and to manage issues that have been escalated.

✅ The risks associated with penetration testing can be reduced if the business utilises a qualified and experienced penetration tester (CREST certified), working within the structured constraints of a certified testing company (a CREST member).

Change management

Any changes to the scope of the penetration test (eg. additional testing requested, such as to include wireless or device testing); or to organisational controls (eg. to address a critical weakness uncovered during testing) need to be managed quickly and efficiently. Consequently, a change management system should be applied to any changes to the testing scope or the configuration of target systems.

Problem resolution

Problems (and complaints) can arise during the test, for example due to resources not being made available, tests not working as planned or a breach of a code of conduct. It is therefore important to ensure that there is a problem resolution process in place to ensure that any issues are resolved satisfactorily, in a timely manner.

CREST members – and the penetration testers they employ – are required to adhere to rigorous codes of conduct for both the individual testers and the organisations for who they work; backed up by an independent investigation scheme should conflicts arise. Details of these codes are available from CREST at: *http://www.crest-approved.org/crest-member-companies/code-of-conduct/index.html*

Overview

When conducting a penetration test it is essential to use a systematic, structured methodology. There are several different open source penetration testing methodologies, with the two most commonly adopted ones described in the:

- Open Source Security Testing Methodology Manual (OSSTM) for infrastructure testing;
- Open Web Application Security Project (OWASP) for web application testing.

✅ The main publicly available methodologies are outlined in the following box entitled **Penetration testing initiatives.**

Leading suppliers are fully aware of all the main methodologies, but often feel they are not comprehensive enough. Consequently, most of these suppliers have developed their own methodologies, but are able to show compliance to other 'standard' methodologies if required.

✅ Any methodology should merely be a guideline. The actual testers often spend considerable time trying to hack into a system using any method they can, and the good ones develop the most appropriate (informal) methodology that each scenario demands.

Broadly, all forms of penetration testing adhere to some variant of the process shown in *Figure 7*; and tests should progress through each of these steps in order. The activities performed and amount of time spent on each step will vary depending on the nature of the test, the scope agreed prior to testing and the target system.

Figure 7: A typical penetration testing process

✅ In many tests, step 2-4 will be repeated a number of times.

Penetration testing initiatives
There are a number of penetration testing initiatives being produced by collaborative (often open or free source) bodies. These initiatives include security assessment frameworks or standards; testing processes, structures or approaches; and useful sources of information about testing techniques and common vulnerabilities. Some of the main penetration testing initiatives are summarised as follows:

OSSTM
The Open Source Security Testing Methodology Manual (OSSTMM) is a peer-reviewed methodology for performing security tests and using metrics. The OSSTMM focuses on the technical details of exactly which items need to be tested, what to do before, during and after a security test, and how to measure the results. OSSTMM is also known for its *Rules of Engagement* which define for both the tester and the client how the test needs to be properly run, starting from denying false advertising from testers to how the client can expect to receive the report. New tests for international best practices, laws, regulations and ethical concerns are regularly added and updated.

OWASP
The Open Web Application Security Project (OWASP) is an open community dedicated to enabling organisations to develop, purchase and

maintain applications that can be trusted. All of the OWASP tools, documents, forums and chapters are free and open to anyone interested in improving application security. They advocate approaching application security as a people, process and technology (PPT) problem because the most effective approaches to application security include improvements in all of these areas.

NIST

The National Institute of Standards and Technology (NIST) mentions penetration testing in SP800- 115.[3]. NIST's methodology is less comprehensive than the OSSTMM; however, it is more likely to be accepted by regulatory agencies. For this reason, NIST refers to the OSSTMM.

ISSAF

The *Information Systems Security Assessment Framework (ISSAF)* is a peer-reviewed structured framework from the *Open Information Systems Security Group* that categorises information system security assessment into various domains and details specific evaluation or testing criteria for each of these domains. It aims to provide field inputs on security assessment that reflect real life scenarios. The ISSAF is, however, still in its infancy.

PTES

The *Penetration Testing Execution Standard (PTES)* is an emerging standard being produced by a reputable group of volunteer penetration testing specialists. It is designed to provide both businesses and security service providers with a common language and scope for performing penetration testing (ie. security evaluations).

Carry out planning

A detailed test plan should be produced that outlines what will actually be done during the test itself, often as series of discrete tasks. This plan should identify the processes, techniques or procedures to be used during the test.

The test plan provides a mechanism for formally agreeing the testing scope and all activities which surround the testing. This is very important so that both parties can ensure that their needs are met and that the terms of reference for the testing activities are clear.

✔ The test plan should be produced by the testing supplier and agreed with the customer prior to any testing commencing.

*'A good test plan helps to assure the process for a
proper security test without creating misunderstandings,
misconceptions, or false expectations'*

Conduct research

The objective is to try and imitate the research activities that a potential attacker could undertake to find out as much about the target environment and how it works as possible. Typical techniques are described in the table below.

Technique	Description
Information gathering	Collating and analysing information about the target, often available from public sources of information, including the Internet. This can provide considerable detail about an organisation, including its technology environment, type of business and security structure.
Reconnaissance	Obtaining positive confirmation of information about the target. Contact is made with the organisation to confirm that system configuration and security controls are as expected. Examples include: visiting a target site as a guest or bystander to confirm physical details and sending traffic to confirm the existence of routers, web servers and email servers.
Network enumeration / scanning	Establishing the potential points of access being offered by a target. In a network test this can involve scanning for open services on targets or establishing the existence of possible user identification credentials.
Discovery and assessment	Learning about a target's infrastructure (eg. by foot printing, mining blogs or using search engines and social networking sites) and determining how the target system works.

Identify vulnerabilities

The objective is to identify a range of potential vulnerabilities in a target system, which will typically involve the tester examining:

- attack avenues, vectors and threat agents (eg. using attack trees);
- results from threat analysis;
- technical system / network / application vulnerabilities;
- control weaknesses.

The types of testing carried out should include automated attack methodologies (eg. scanning), manual testing (experimenting with numerous tools) and additional techniques (eg. artificial intelligence, enabling higher number of iterations of attack to be performed).

✅ Most testers will include a review of vulnerabilities identified by third parties, such as the 'OWASP Top Ten, which presents a list of common security vulnerabilities found in web applications (ie. injection attacks, cross-site scripting and failure to restrict URL access).

'Many vulnerabilities that we detect result from a lack of understanding of IT security issues; certainly from web developers and users of mobile devices, which is often the greatest threat'

Exploit weaknesses

Once vulnerabilities have been identified in the target environment, testers will use exploitation frameworks, stand-alone exploits and other tactics to try and take advantage of these weaknesses (eg. using precision strikes or customised exploitation) to actually penetrate the target system.

The types of technique typically employed are outlined in the following table.

Technique	Description
Exploit	Using identified vulnerabilities to gain unauthorised access to the target. For example, in a web application test, this may involve injecting commands into the application that provide a level of control over the target. Exploitation may require the combination of several sets of information in a creative way.

Technique	Description
Escalation	Gaining further access within a target, once an initial level of access has been obtained. For example, in a network test, successful exploitation may allow user or guest access to a system. Escalation through additional exploitation will typically be required to obtain administrative privilege.
Advancement	Attempting to move on from the compromised target to find other vulnerable systems. For example, in a network test this will consist of 'hopping' from one system to another, potentially using the access obtained on the original target to access other systems. In a physical test, this might involve moving from one compromised building to another.
Analysis	Analysing and verifying the raw data to ensure that the test has been thorough and comprehensive. Depending upon the environment, consultants may conduct additional manual tests. They will then interpret the results to produce a tailored, business-focused report.

Report findings

Findings identified during the penetration test should be recorded in an agreed format describing each finding in both:

- Technical terms that can be acted upon;

- Non -technical, business context, so that the justifications for the corrective actions are understood.

Reports should describe the vulnerabilities found, including:

- Test narrative – describing the process that the tester used to achieve particular results;

- Test evidence – results of automated testing tools and screen shots of successful exploits;

- The associated technical risks – and how to address them.

✔ It is often helpful to ensure that suppliers use a common reporting template, enabling you to compare results from different tests and from different providers.

Once the report has been digested internally and notes taken a presentation should be arranged with your supplier to present the results, highlighting:

- how they found the vulnerabilities;
- what could be the outcome of each vulnerability;
- the level of risk to the business;
- remediation advice.

Remediate

After the test is complete it is often the responsibility of your test manager to ensure that the results are acted upon. The report should be disseminated to the relevant staff and the remediation of the identified vulnerabilities and associated 'root causes' should begin.

Overview

Once the penetration test is complete – and any specifically identified vulnerabilities have been addressed – it can be tempting to draw a line under the process and return to business as usual. However, to reduce risks both in the longer term and across the whole organisation, it is often useful to initiate an improvement programme. An example of such a programme is shown in *Figure 8*.

Root causes

The real root causes of exposures – not just the symptoms of an attack – should be identified and their potential impact on the business evaluated. To identify more endemic or fundamental 'root causes', you may require your supplier to involve qualified, experienced security professionals to help define corrective action strategy and plans.

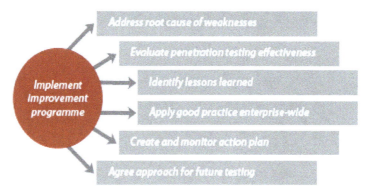

Figure 8: Key elements in the production of a scope statement

Penetration testing effectiveness

The effectiveness of the penetration test should be evaluated to help determine if objectives were met and that value for money has been obtained from your supplier. This can also help in planning future tests and provides valuable feedback to suppliers to help them improve processes.

Lessons learned

The lessons learned during the penetration testing approach – and the test itself – should be identified and recorded, to avoid weaknesses recurring.

Several suppliers interviewed said that they uncovered the same security issues at the same client on a number of occasions, possibly because the client has only fixed the problem in the particular environment being tested. If trend analysis is performed, this can reveal in quantitative terms that this was the case, which is likely to encourage the client to address the problem.

Good practice

When addressing the weaknesses identified in an environment, good practices identified (including fixes) should be highlighted – and applied to a wide range of other environments. This can be achieved by:

- Performing trend analysis across multiple systems;
- Applying lessons learnt during a penetration test of one application to similar applications;
- Fixing root causes endemically.

Action plan

A plan should be produced, outlining all the relevant actions to be taken to prevent vulnerabilities identified through testing from recurring, and to help improve the overall information security programme. This action plan should include the following details for each action identified:

- brief description of action;
- category and priority of action;
- individuals responsible and accountable for the action;
- target date for completion.

The action plan should then be monitored on a regular basis to ensure progress is being made and to highlight any delays or difficulties being experienced.

Future testing

When considering how, when and what to test in the future, analysis of the results from previous penetration tests can be very useful.

PART IV: CHOOSING A SUITABLE SUPPLIER

Introduction

If your organisation decides to appoint an external provider of penetration services, it is important that you choose a supplier who can most effectively meet your requirements, but at the right price.

This part of the Guide will help your organisation to:
1. Review your penetration testing requirements;
2. Define a set of supplier selection criteria;
3. Identify possible suppliers to be considered;
4. Select an appropriate supplier who can meet (or exceed) your requirements.

> *'What we are looking for from a supplier is certainty, prioritisation, trust and security'*

A. Review requirements

The first step is to make sure that whoever chooses the supplier fully understands your organisation's requirements, and is aware of any necessary management, planning and preparation activities. Much of this should be determined in the requirements stage of the procurement approach, but will be vital in procuring the right service from the most appropriate supplier.

✔ You should consider who is driving the relationship with the supplier within your organisation. It is seldom a good idea to just leave it to a corporate procurement person, as this is unlikely to deliver maximum value. From interviews with service providers, when clients have used a security or compliance person to drive the relationship, this has typically produced better results.

The chosen supplier should fully understand each of the stages in the procurement approach outlined in the previous parts of this Guide. Consequently, they should be able to help you:
1. Understand and meet business requirements, which include defining business drivers, identifying target systems and determining the purpose of the test;

2. Produce a scope statement, which includes the testing style (eg. white or black box testing) the testing type (eg. web application or infrastructure) and any testing constraints;

3. Establish a management assurance framework, which includes an assurance process, contractual agreement, change management, risk mitigation and problem resolution;

4. Plan for and conduct the actual penetration test in a competent, professional manner;

5. Help you initiate an effective improvement programme.

'It is important to ensure that the right systems are being tested by the right people for the right reasons at the right time'

⚠ Some organisations seem to believe that they just need a 'tick in the box' and may be looking for a 'cheap and dirty' solution. However, this often does not produce required results and may even create a false sense of security. It can also cause difficulties during the procurement process as quality suppliers will believe in doing a proper test.

Other considerations

In addition to defined business requirements and an agreed scope statement, there may be other considerations when selecting a supplier. For example, your organisation may have a well-established (or preferential) relationship with a particular supplier or a need to appoint (or reject) an organisation for commercial or political reasons.

⚠ When appointing external suppliers – for any purpose – you will sometimes have to take account of topics covering political, legal/regulatory, socio-economic and technological (PLEST) issues.

Furthermore, your requirements can be influenced by the size (and bargaining power) of your organisation and the market sectors in which your organisation operates. For example, the following case study outlines what a large international bank can require of their suppliers.

CASE STUDY – *BANKING*

An interview with an individual responsible for the procurement of penetration testing in a large international bank explained that they have a wide and deep set of requirements for their suppliers. Aside from the standard 'procurement style' requirements (eg. about good reputation, capability and fitness for purpose) that go into a Request for Proposal (RFP), they are looking for suppliers to:

- Be flexible, so that they can react to an incident very quickly, but still in a highly competent manner – as well as deal with special requirements for out of hours testing;

- Conduct pre-employment screening (PES) of employees (including analysis of CV, background checks, security clearance), which the bank will then carry out a sample check of to see what has been done;

- Evidence that their testers are renowned in the industry, for example by checking speaking engagements, research published and general activity in the community;

- Deliver *'absolute quality',* ensuring that their testers identify all significant vulnerabilities and know how to fix them;

- Use pro-formas for testing, but tailored to meet specific needs, producing a detailed list of tasks to be performed;

- Monitor the penetration test and check the results, focusing on why a particular vulnerability was missed (with an audit trail) – and the bank may get a second supplier to check this;

- Retain all records of the testing performed for seven years, with spot checks on this, too.

This bank was also looking for suppliers to explain exactly what their penetration testing comprises, including their:

- capabilities (often globally)

- proformas available (and what they are for);

- assessments methodologies – which should take into account reviews by 'black hat' IT specialists (and be marked by multiple people);

- tools deployed, both for testing and reporting;

- provision of tailoring services;

- recording methods, showing what they did and to what – providing a reliable audit trail of evidence.

B. Define supplier selection criteria

Depending on individual requirements, many organisations are looking for a supplier who can:

- Provide a reliable, effective and proven penetration testing service;
- Meet compliance standards and the requirements of corporate or government policy, protecting client information and systems both during and after testing;
- Perform rigorous and effective penetration tests, ensuring that a wide range of system attacks are simulated – using a proven testing methodology;
- Discover all major vulnerabilities, identify associated 'root causes' and strategically analyse key findings in business terms;
- Co-develop security improvement strategies and programmes, recommending countermeasures to both address vulnerabilities and prevent them from recurring;
- Produce insightful, practical and easy to read reports, engaging with senior management in business terms, resolving issues with IT service providers and addressing global risk management issues;
- Provide on-going advice on how to manage systems effectively over time as part of a trusted relationship.

'Our supplier is a trusted organisation who employs competent people – and this combination is important'

To ensure that your chosen supplier will meet your requirements it can be helpful to define a set of supplier criteria, most of which your chosen supplier should be able to meet – or exceed. The six main criteria typically considered are outlined in *Figure 9* and described in more detail throughout the rest of this part of the Guide.

Supplier selection criteria

1. Solid reputation, history and ethics
2. High quality, value-for-money services
3. Research and development capability
4. Highly competent, technical resters
5. Security and risk management
6. Strong professional accreditation and complaint process

Figure 9: Key selection criteria for choosing a suitable supplier of penetration testing services

You should determine which of the areas described need to be incorporated into your own, tailored set of supplier selection criteria and record these in a document that can be passed to potential suppliers – and your procurement department – sometimes as part of an RFP (Request for Proposal).

✅ There are many benefits in procuring penetration testing services from a trusted, certified external company who employ professional, ethical and highly technically competent individuals. CREST member companies are certified penetration testing organisations that fully meet this requirement, have been awarded the gold standard in penetration testing and build trusted relationships with their clients.

---

1. Solid reputation, history and ethics

Two of the most important criteria for a buyer of penetration testing services to consider are the reputation (and history) of the supplier and the ethical conduct they adopt (and enforce).

When assessing the **reputation** of a potential penetration testing supplier you should ensure that they:

- Have a full trading history, with a reliable financial record and a strong history of performance;

- Maintain a good reputation both with clients and across the industry – obtaining independent feedback from clients about their performance;

- Have an active involvement in the community (eg. by sharing findings within their own networks) – and hold relevant corporate memberships;

- Show evidence of lessons that they have learned being applied both to their clients and in the wider community;

- Can resolve technical issues (eg. with IT service providers), yet also address global risk management issues;

- Provide additional management and technical support services;

- Carry adequate indemnity insurance.

When reviewing the **ethical posture** adhered to by a potential penetration testing supplier you should ensure that the supplier:
- Achieves suitable professional accreditation (such as CREST);

- Is a member of current, relevant professional and industry bodies;

- Employs professional, qualified and well-trained individuals with appropriate clearances;

- Adheres to an approved 'code of conduct', which applies to both the organisation itself and the individuals involved with the test;
- Obtains independent feedback on the quality of work performed and conduct of staff involved;
- Has processes in place for agreeing scope and obtaining permissions for the type of work to be conducted, where it will take place and what information and systems will be accessed;
- Acts in an ethical manner and helps vendors to fix problems;
- Has an effective hiring, vetting and on-boarding processes for penetration testers – providing appropriate career development.

✅ CREST provides organisations wishing to buy penetration testing services with confidence that they can procure services from a CREST member company safe in the knowledge that each member has been independently assessed (and re-audited every year) to ensure that they:

- Carry out stringent background checks on their staff;
- Provide their staff with a structured framework covering awareness, education, research and career development;
- Deploy rigorous testing methodologies and processes;
- Produce clear, insightful reports for both technical and management audiences;
- Protect client information in a professional manner;
- Meet any legal, regulatory or business constraints on their testing;
- Have signed company and individual codes of conduct;
- Adhere to a signed memorandum of agreement on good practice;
- Deal with complaints in a diligent fashion, with agreement that any conflict can be handled by an independent professional body.

---

2. High quality, value-for-money services

Some suppliers will hit you with a volley of 'vendor hype' that can be difficult to penetrate. It can therefore be a real challenge to find the right quality of service at the right price.

⚠ There can be a big difference between a cheap penetration testing service and one that provides real value for money. For example, many low cost services may not provide certified, professional staff that can uncover and address significant vulnerabilities or act in an ethical manner according to defined code of conduct. Furthermore, there is typically little recourse in the event of a dispute (eg. no independent adjudication and sometimes not even any indemnity insurance).

---

*'If you have been compelled to conduct a penetration test,
then our penetration testing services may not be for you, but
if you want to conduct a proper test, give us a call'*

When determining the **quality of the services** provided by a potential penetration testing supplier you should ensure that the supplier:

- Maintains quality management and audit systems (including security requirements), sample content and templates (sometimes used by clients to help develop RFPs);

- Has a quality assurance process that applies to each test being undertaken, to help make sure client requirements are being met in a secure, productive manner;

- Can deal with the management aspects relating to test set-up;

- Provides clear, insightful reporting, presented both for technical specialists and business representatives;

- Is able to quantify findings and link them to possible impacts on your business, possibly supported by some sort of traffic light system (or equivalent) to show severity;

- Issues an assurance report upon which third parties can place reliance;

- Follows-through with a security improvement programme to address the fundamental 'root causes.

A high quality supplier can differentiate themselves from competitors by the quality of the customer services they provide, which can be very successful for retaining existing clients (because they can see the quality), but more tricky for new clients as other providers will often claim the same thing.

*'A good penetration testing supplier will provide a
professional service wrapper around the test'*

When determining the **effectiveness of the testing process** used by a potential penetration testing supplier you should ensure that the supplier:

- Employs a proven testing methodology, which is tailored for particular types of environment (eg. infrastructure, web applications, mobile computing) – and is kept up-to-date;

- Can evaluate the whole target environment and not just a particular system;

- Will design and execute a test tailored to your needs;

- Carries out full penetration tests (subject to the scope statement), rather than just running a set of automated tests using standard tools.

🛈 An individual may be a highly competent penetration tester, with great technical ability, but may not have good management consultancy skills. A good penetration testing supplier will provide greater attention to client needs, with business-focused customer service and more actionable components to their testing methodology.

When appointing a supplier, the client can benefit from the supplier providing additional services, such as:

- intrusion analysis: evaluating attempted and successful breaches;

- incident response: classifying, containing and responding to security incidents – and identifying their root causes;

- reverse engineering of attacks;

- security architecture: helping to design and implement a more resilient infrastructure for your organisation;

- security management.

✅ Some suppliers will provide assistance in interpreting the results of a previous penetration test – or an audit. A cost benefit analysis performed by the supplier might identify this (or similar activities) as a way for you to reduce audit costs.

Depending on your requirements, you may need a supplier who can meet specific requirements, such as those specified in the following table.

If you want to....	Look for a supplier who can provide a...
Employ a penetration tester at short notice	Qualified tester almost immediately, as some suppliers have lead times up to several weeks. It is usually better to wait for the right suitably qualified person, as to procure the services of an unqualified tester because of a critical business need makes little sense.
Handle the needs of large, sophisticated organisations operating on an international basis	True global capability, employing a pragmatic approach across multiple systems and environments.

On an international basis, the inconsistent use of jargon makes the procurement of consistently high quality services even more difficult. As with other professions, internationally recognised qualifications (or equivalent) are one of the only true measures of professional, quality services.

The need for professional, quality services
There is a vast difference between a CREST certified tester – with more than 10,000 hours regular, practical experience, who has had their knowledge tested every three years by their industry peers – compared to a tester who has attended a one week course and passed a test as a Certified Ethical Hacker (CEH).

There is room in the industry for both levels and CEH can provide a good grounding – but the company procuring the service must understand the difference and appoint an appropriate supplier in line with their requirements.

Professional, quality services are now becoming available in a growing number of countries. But even if you are operating in a country where there is no professional body and very limited relevant professional qualifications, you should still ask for them as this will help to increase the likelihood of them being made available in the future. If sufficient numbers of buyers are asking for demonstrable quality services the industry will slowly react thereby improving the level of services to everyone –all across the world.

If no one asks for professional, quality services then the supplier industry will have little reason to invest in improvements in processes and controls or the skills, knowledge and competence of their staff. By requesting quality services, you may even be supporting internal requests for investment within the supplier community by individuals who have invested the time and effort in their own personal development.

You can make a difference!

3. Research and development capability

One of the biggest selling points for some suppliers is the quality and depth of their technical research and development (R&D) capability. When determining the *quality of the R&D services* provided by a potential penetration testing supplier you should ensure that the supplier:
• Publishes vulnerabilities (in the right place, at an appropriate time);

- Is active in the technical community (eg. part of a cyber-intelligence team);
- Provides comprehensive on-going threat analysis, by performing their own research and evaluating a wide range of threat sources, such as the:
  - SANS annual top 20 list of Internet security vulnerabilities;
  - OWASP ten most critical web application security risks;
- Considers all stage of a potential cybercrime attack, which typically comprises reconnaissance, development of attack, extraction of information, exploitation of information and money laundering;
- Carries out sufficient research and development activities to be able to identify all significant vulnerabilities (eg. broken authentication and session management, insecure Direct Object References, failure to restrict URL access or insufficient Transport Layer protection);
- Constantly develops specific methodologies to address different environments such as infrastructure, web application, wireless, mobile etc.;
- Does not just use a standard set of tools – but carries out specially tailored, manual tests to help detect unknown vulnerabilities.

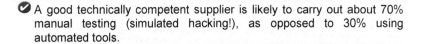 A good technically competent supplier is likely to carry out about 70% manual testing (simulated hacking!), as opposed to 30% using automated tools.

Some suppliers will also:

- Develop and deploy the technical and architectural improvements necessary to reduce exposure to both internal and external threats;
- Have state-of-the-art research and development facilities (eg. specialised laboratories or centres of excellence) where they continuously research the latest threats, techniques and countermeasures;
- Align penetration testing with other forms of security testing or monitoring.

✅ Some suppliers can provide automated tools for recording and presenting key aspects of a penetration test, often using a management dashboard (often with drill-down capabilities). These tools can allow the client to monitor a range of parameters, such as:

- attack characteristics (eg. attack types, attack vectors and attack trees);
- the number and type of vulnerabilities (including chains of vulnerabilities);
- the business impact of exploits;
- severity of vulnerabilities and the relationship with disaster conditions.

4. Highly competent, technical testers

In such a highly specialised field suppliers need to be able to provide penetration testers who are proficient in many domains of security, have an extensive knowledge of network devices and infrastructure and are an expert in web and server programming languages. Individual penetration testers need to be able to be able to demonstrate that they:

- Have relevant technical capability in the various areas in which tests may be required (such as application testing);
- Maintain an up-to-date knowledge of the latest threats and countermeasures – and are given sufficient time to do research;
- Can program in a fairly low level language (not necessarily code review, as this is often too time consuming);
- Identify 'root cause' findings, strategically analyse findings in business terms, and co-develop security improvement strategies and programmes;
- Understand the business implications of technical weaknesses or exploits.

❗ There is a risk when carrying out a penetration test that security can be compromised or the performance or availability of key systems adversely affected. A professional and trained tester will be able mitigate these risks, whereas an inexperienced or untrained individual may not.

The penetration testers used by your supplier should have deep, technical capabilities in the specific areas that are relevant to your target environment (eg. web application, infrastructure, mobile or vendor-specific). Expertise should be relevant to the type of test being carried out, rather than just virtually unlimited technical expertise.

'Put the right people on the right job at the right time'

CREST provides accreditation in different technical areas, such as CREST web application testers and CREST infrastructure testers. There are also specific examinations in areas such as wireless testing.

One of the key points when managing testers is to understand what they cannot do. An individual penetration tester – however talented – is unlikely to be an expert in all the different flavours of networks, operating systems and application software, particularly those provided by vendors. Consequently:

- It can help if they are part of a larger capability – or network – where they can draw on the experience of others;

- When it comes to testing of specific vendor software, suppliers should be able to sub-contract to other more specialist vendors, if required.

By imitating the client environment at a supplier's site (such as in a specialised lab) the testers can tap in to both the technical facilities available and a wider knowledge pool.

A trusted partner (such as those accredited by CREST) will be able to provide assurance that their fully qualified staff will:

- Have achieved the highest possible standards in penetration testing;

- Act in a professional, ethical manner;

- Adopt a structured, systematic and repeatable process;

- Have access to a wider community with the specified aim of sharing and enhancing knowledge;

- Bring with them a wealth of experience drawn from client work across a range of companies and sectors allowing lesson learnt to be transferred;

- Provide constructive, expert remediation advice;

- Ensure that the results of tests are generated, reported, stored, communicated and destroyed in a manner that does not put the organisation at risk.

✅ CREST certified testers are required to:

- Have gained five years practical full time experience;
- Be part of an on-going professional development programme;
- Undertake very technically demanding regular assessment;
- Re-take all their examinations (the content changes often) every three years.

Even at the CREST Registered tester level, two years practical full time experience is normally required – following on from relevant technical experience or specialised MSc courses – to pass the required technical assessment.

5. Security and risk management

It is important that the supplier themselves is secure – and has a positive approach to both security and risk. Your supplier should be able to provide assurances – preferably in writing – that the security and risks associated with your critical systems and confidential information (together with any other business risks) are being adequately addressed.

During any security assessment it is likely that the test team will encounter sensitive or business critical data. You will need to be comfortable that you can trust both the supplier – and every individual tester they provide.

✅ In order to carry out effective penetration testing, the tester must be methodical and technically competent. The CREST scheme requires organisations supporting that tester to demonstrate that they have appropriate procedures and controls in place to protect client information and systems. These organisations are also subject to regular (annual) independent audits to ensure the highest standards continue to be achieved.

The *risk management processes* of a provider should be clearly understood before a test is undertaken. Your supplier should be able to explain how:

- Tools and methodologies are tested before being used in live tests;
- Their operational risk management works during a test;
- Information (including test results) is kept secure;
- They take ownership of and guide client management in their own internal risk management;

- Individuals involved with the test are subject to security background checks before being permitted to perform testing;
- Tools utilised as part of a test will not themselves introduce additional risks;
- Results of tests are generated, reported, stored, communicated and destroyed in a manner that does not put the organisation at risk.

---

❶ Although a supplier may be accredited (eg. through ISO27001, or similar), the scope of this accreditation needs to be checked as it is often only for a particular part or function of an organisation (eg. an on-line banking system or a data centre).

Security requirements should be included by the supplier in contracts (also a requirement of ISO27002, section 6.2), which ideally should state the way in which specific tasks will be undertaken, include provision of a security template and specify responsibilities of both the buyer and supplier.

---

❶ During some penetration tests there can be problems with the scope of the test, which can result in compromises of security for:

- staff or clients of the organisation being tested;
- other organisations altogether.

It is therefore critical that your supplier obtains formal approval to carry out tests from all relevant management in your organisation that may be affected by the tests and from any other connected organisations or individuals. You should be concerned if your supplier does not specifically ask for these signed approvals.

---

6. Strong professional accreditation and complaint process

Penetration testing organisations who have been professionally accredited will provide you with confidence that major vulnerabilities have been identified and properly addressed. They will also bring with them a wealth of experience drawn from client work across a range of companies and sectors, allowing lessons learnt from one to be transferred to others.

Utilising a supplier that has been independently audited regarding the manner in which their tests are carried out and the way in which company information is handled will also provide a much greater level of confidence in the testing carried out.

Appointing suppliers that are members of a professional penetration testing body, such as CREST, can provide you with a reliable and proven complaint process, including constructive advice. So if there are any problems with the quality of work done or the approach taken by the testers, you can rest assured that an expert and independent body is on hand to investigate any complaint thoroughly and ensure that a satisfactory conclusion is reached.

There are a number of different accreditation schemes available that apply to penetration testing, both for individual penetration testers and for organisations who provide penetration testing services. These schemes are often designed to meet different requirements and provide varying levels of assurance.

✅ Where UK Government systems (eg. those handling protectively marked information) are to be tested the supplier selection process may be narrowed, as all such providers are required to be members of the CHECK scheme. Further information on CHECK can be found at: *www.cesg.gov.uk/site/check/index.cfm*

For optimal results, the *accredited body* used by your supplier should provide:
- Stringent criteria for suppliers to become members, backed up by regular (eg. annual) assessments;
- Rigorous examination criteria for individual penetration testers, including specialised examinations for web application and infrastructure testing;
- Methods of helping their members to improve penetration testing and methodologies;

- An independent client feedback process to encourage improvements in client service and to enable comparison to be made;
- A code of conduct for both member organisations and the penetration testers they employ, to ensure ethical, professional behaviour and approaches;
- A constructive, expert complaint process, with sufficient independence and authority to resolve issues.

🔴 Make sure that your supplier is a member of an organisation that can provide an expert, reputable and independent complaint process.

A CREST member can expect to receive severe penalties if they do not act in a professional, ethical manner. They can have their accreditation removed if they do not meet required standards or have proven in an investigation to have been significantly negligent or unethical. In the worst case, this could result in a significant reduction in business, as clients would not be prepared to employ their services.

The following case study illustrates the response from an organisation to the way in which CREST carried out an independent investigation into a complaint about a particular penetration testing provider, who is a member of CREST.

CASE STUDY – *FEEDBACK ON THE CREST COMPLAINT PROCESS*

'We discussed your report in detail in our Information Security Committee and fed back our thoughts to our Executive Committee, which includes all executive directors. The unanimous view was that your report was fair, accurate and had addressed the major concerns that we had with this project.

We were pleased to see that you agreed a package of sensible controls with our supplier and, based on the information available to us, we believe that these are proportionate and appropriate. As far as we are concerned, the matter is now closed.

Overall, I think that CREST gets a thumbs-up from us for the way that this was addressed. We would obviously have preferred to have never found ourselves in the position that we were in, but, given that things had gone wrong, your complaints process appears to have worked well on this occasion.'

In some cases, organisations are accredited themselves but do not use accredited individuals to conduct your penetration test, so the required quality of testing may not be achieved. In other cases, an individual may be accredited but does not work for an accredited organisation, meaning that there are fewer assurances and any complaint may be difficult to resolve.

🛈 The optimum combination is shown in the green box in *Figure 10*. This is the only combination that provides you with a tangible level of protection should things go wrong – and also reduces the likelihood of a problem occurring in the first place.

ORGANISATION

Figure 10: Combinations of accreditation for organisations and the individuals they employ

Although value can be obtained by appointing either certified testers or certified organisations, it is the combination of these that will provide you with the greatest assurance that the most effective tests will be conducted – and in the most professional manner.

Furthermore, by procuring penetration testing services from certified testers who work for certified organisations (as CREST require), you can rest assured that an expert and independent body – with real authority – is on hand to investigate any complaint thoroughly and ensure that a satisfactory conclusion is reached

'CREST provides demonstrable assurance of the processes and procedures of member organisations and validates the competence of information security testers'

C. Identify potential suppliers

It can often be difficult to produce a short list of potential suppliers, not least because there are so many to choose from. For example, penetration testing suppliers can include:

- Organisations specialising in penetration testing (often small boutique firms);
- Information security consultancies and integrators, with penetration testing teams;

- Systems integrators and outsourcing service providers with penetration testing teams;
- Regulated professional services firms, including the 'Big 4' accountancy firms, with penetration testing teams.

To help identify potential suppliers, you may wish to carry out some background research to see if they have:

- Carried out the type of testing you require;
- Received positive feedback from previous clients;
- Taken part in specialised industry events, such as those run by CREST or OWASP chapters;
- Produced research papers, published vulnerabilities or won awards in the industry;
- Valid accreditations and qualifications;
- Membership of a professional penetration testing body, such as CREST;
- Complied with appropriate vetting standards (eg. BS7858, or equivalent);
- Been audited (eg. by some of their larger clients), to provide assurance for their wider client base.

Get a recommendation or reference

If you have colleagues or industry peers you can trust, seek out their advice and request them to recommend a suitable supplier. You should talk to the referee directly and ask them questions like:

- Do you still use this supplier?
- How long have you been using them?
- Would you consider changing?
- What are their strengths?
- What are their weaknesses?

Make sure the referee has actually used the supplier they are recommending and acquired a service similar to the one you require – for the same type of target environment.

Evaluate potential suppliers

It is often important to validate the credentials of the suppliers you wish to consider – taking into account your supplier selection criteria. As part of

67

the validation process, you should consider asking your potential suppliers to:

- Make a presentation of their capabilities;
- Show examples of similar (sanitised) projects they have undertaken;
- Provide a sample report – and then evaluate its quality and clarity;
- Respond to an RFP (or a just a scope statement if a smaller client) – and make sure they either meet or exceed requirements.

✅ Consider inviting suppliers to test something at the same time as their competitors, but without informing any supplier involved. You can then compare the quality or results achieved and the level of service provided.

If you represent a particularly large organisation – or have significant testing requirements – you could also ask potential suppliers to take part in a 'dry run' test, conducted with several other suppliers. This might involve asking a range of different vendors to:

- Take a test – or even sit an exam;
- Carry out an assessment on a test system that has deliberate vulnerabilities built in;
- Write up their findings in a suitable manner, so that you can understand the nature and content of the vulnerabilities, their business impact and how to fix them;
- Tell you explicitly what to do to remediate particular weaknesses (eg. for a particular software version).

✅ Large organisations may also choose to invite competitive tenders from penetration testing providers to be on a 'call-off' contract framework. They then call off work against it, perhaps re-tendering the providers on the framework for larger penetration tests.

The individual performing the penetration test must not test anything beyond the agreed scope, to do so would be unethical – and, in some cases, illegal. Consequently, a great deal of trust will be placed in the individual penetration testers that you employ.

To reduce this risk, you can:

- Check the professional certifications of a sample of testers – and their depth of experience;
- Examine background checks suppliers perform on their employees – and validate a sample - for example to identify criminals, ex-hackers or other potentially unsuitable individuals;

- Review the track record of the test team to see who they have worked with and in what capacity;
- Exercise your right to reject particular individuals.

❶ CVs of individual testers, and confirmation of their qualifications, can be sent to you upon request – another way of highlighting their competence. However, this can be a double-edged sword as the supplier may have to provide alternative testers if named individuals are otherwise engaged.

D. Select appropriate supplier(s)

After carefully considering all the relevant supplier selection criteria – and evaluating potential suppliers – you will then need to formally appoint one or more suppliers. The key consideration should still be to select a supplier who can help you meet your specific requirements – at the right price – not just one who can offer a variety of often impressive products and services, some of which may not necessarily be relevant.

❶ Prior to work starting, arrangements with your chosen supplier should be satisfactorily detailed in a contract signed off by both parties, as defined in **Part 3, Stage 3 Management assurance framework.**

Supplier appointment models

The appointment and continued use of external providers can be managed in a number of ways that can be tailored to fit an organisation's style. Use of penetration testing providers tends to fall into the following models.

Supplier appointment model	Advantages	Disadvantages
Single provision A single provider is used for all penetration testing.	This can provide an extensive relationship where the supplier is very familiar with your organisation and can therefore provide insightful and practical recommendations.	A single supplier may not be able to provide all types of penetration testing equally well. In addition, over-familiarity may give rise to conflicts of interest.

Supplier appointment model	Advantages	Disadvantages
Dual provision Two suppliers are used. Penetration tests are assigned according to the technical speciality of the supplier (eg. one supplier for infrastructure testing and one for application testing).	This retains the benefits of single provision while also playing to the strengths of the providers.	The possibility of over-familiarity remains with this model, and there may be additional cost associated with suppliers having to gain background information on the target systems.
Testing panel Multiple suppliers are used. Penetration tests are either assigned in a cyclic fashion or according to technical speciality.	Over-familiarity is less of a possibility and subsequent penetration tests on systems can be performed by different providers to make testing more thorough.	The selection, contract maintenance and test management can be complex and expensive.
Ad-hoc Various suppliers are used, dependent on the particular penetration test being performed.	This model allows for flexibility and the ability to specifically select suppliers based on their capability.	Suppliers are likely to have little or no familiarity with systems.

Some organisations choose to rotate vendors, with a timescale dependent on the type and number of tests to be performed.

✅ Tests are often carried out on a regular (typically annual) basis. However, they are often more effective if carried out immediately before (or after) a major change – often saving money in the longer run, too.

CREST BALANCED SCORECARD

Company Membership

Demonstrable level of assurance of processes and procedures of member organisations.

Knowledge Sharing

Guidance and standards. Opportunity to share and enhance knowledge.

Professional Qualifications

Validate the competence of information security professionals.

Professional Development

Encourage talent into the market. On-going personal development.

For further information contact CREST at *www.crest-approved.org*

EU for product safety is Stephen Evans, The Mill Enterprise Hub, Stagreenan, Drogheda, Co. Louth, A92 CD3D, Ireland. (servicecentre@itgovernance.eu)

www.ingramcontent.com/pod-product-compliance
Lightning Source LLC
LaVergne TN
LVHW012333060326
832902LV00011B/1869